On My Mind

Aa'Shauntae Chapman

India | USA | UK

On My Mind © 2024 Aa'Shauntae Chapman

All rights reserved.

No part of this publication may be reproduced, stored in a retrieval system, or transmitted, in any form or by any means, electronic, mechanical, photocopying, recording or otherwise, without the prior written permission of the presenters.

Aa'Shauntae Chapman asserts the moral right to be identified as the author of this work.

Presentation by *BookLeaf Publishing*

Web: www.bookleafpub.com

E-mail: info@bookleafpub.com

ISBN: 9789363316546

First edition 2024

*To the whispers yet to thunder, to the quiet
warriors of the unseen struggle, this tome
echoes your subtleties.*

*To the wearers of invisible armor, grappling
with the specters of anxiety, within these pages,
find your haven.*

*To the carriers of silent anguish, may these
verses be a salve to souls and a beacon to guide
you towards serenity.*

*In solidarity with every hushed heartache and
unshed tear, may this poetry amplify your
unspoken truths and offer reprieve.*

Aa'Shauntae Chapman

ACKNOWLEDGEMENT

This book of poetry, a vessel of my innermost thoughts and emotions, would not have been possible without the unwavering support and encouragement of some very special people in my life.

To my cousin Carmen King, your influence and assistance through this journey have been nothing short of transformative. Your insights and suggestions have helped shape my poetry, turning raw emotions into the verses that fill these pages. Your dedication to the art of storytelling has inspired me, and for that, I am eternally grateful. You have been more than a cousin; you have been a mentor, a confidant, and a collaborator in this creative process.

To my mother, Chiquitta Chapman, whose boundless love and patience have never faltered. You have been the audience of first resort, lending an ear to my earliest drafts and offering the encouragement that only a mother can. Your belief in my voice and the stories I strive to tell through poetry has been a source of strength. Thank you for the countless hours spent listening and for the comfort of knowing that you are always there.

To my twin brother, AaShaun Chapman, thank you for being my constant in this ever-changing world. Your encouragement has been the wind beneath the wings of my dreams. You have always believed in my potential, even when I have doubted myself. Your enthusiasm for this project has been infectious, and your conviction that this book could touch lives has driven me to see it through to fruition.

To each of you, my heartfelt thanks. You have been the pillars that have upheld my aspirations, the guiding stars on my poetic journey. Without your love, support, and belief, these pages would remain blank. This book is not only a collection of my poetry but also a testament to the power of family, the beauty of shared dreams, and the unbreakable bonds that enable us to soar.

With deepest gratitude and love,

Aa'Shauntae Chapman

PREFACE

In the quietest hours of the night, when the world hushes its hustle and the stars whisper secrets to the willing mind, a poet picks up a pen. It is in these undisturbed moments that the heart speaks its truths, and from such truths, this collection—On My Mind—was born.

Dear Reader,

You are about to embark on a voyage through the uncharted waters of my psyche. 'On My Mind' is not merely a book of poems; it is a cartography of a soul's landscape, a soul that finds solace in the cadence of words and the rhythm of emotions. Each verse you will encounter is a footprint in the journey of self-discovery, an intimate dance with shadows and light that dwell within us all.

These poems are confidants to the whispers of my spirit, the confessions of my fears, and the declarations of my hopes. They are the silent conversations I have had with the moon, the spirited debates with my reflection, and the tender soliloquies in the embrace of solitude.

This collection is an invitation to witness the rawness of being human, to touch the fabric of feelings often folded away in the recesses of the heart.

In an age where our thoughts are often filtered through the lens of social expectation, 'On My Mind' seeks to break down these barriers. It is a pledge of authenticity, a testament to the courage of laying bare one's inner world. Through these poems, I offer you a mirror, a reflection of the myriad emotions that it is to be alive—the uncertainties, the joys, the sorrows, and the boundless depths of thought.

As you turn these pages, may you find companionship in words, comfort in the shared solitude, and strength in the acknowledgment of your innermost self. This collection is a celebration of the mind's wanderings, the beauty of introspection, and the bravery of those willing to journey through the landscapes of their own thoughts.

May you find within these pages a kindred spirit, and may the journey 'On My Mind' inspire you to embrace the power of your own musings. After all, it is in the quiet acceptance of ourselves that we find the loudest echoes of our truth.

With heartfelt sincerity and an open heart,

Aa'Shauntae Chapman

Order

On my mind, a book of life's stories untold,
A jumbled mess of thoughts both bright and
bold.
Yet in this chaos, there's a pattern that one sees,
A special order of what's on my mind, if you
please.
The memories and dreams, the doubts and fears,
The joys and sorrows, the hopes and tears,
Are all part of the scheme, of what I keep inside,
A story of my life, that I can't hide.
The happy days, the sad ones too,
The moments of doubt, the moments of truth,
All swirl together, in a muddled whirl,
A jumbled mess of emotions, that I must unfurl.
The beauty of this book, of what's on my mind,
Is that the order of it, I can't define.
It's a wild ride, of thoughts and dreams,
That follow no rules, or at least it seems.
So come along, and explore with me,
The randomness of life, in this book of stories.
You can laugh, and you can cry,
You can learn, and you can try,
To make sense of the mess of what's on my
mind.

This is personal

Letting someone into my thoughts,
Is like a bridge I have just crossed
My walls come down, my heart open wide
For this journey, I will not hide

My secrets deep, I keep inside
To share them brings a sense of pride
Vulnerability I can no longer fear
For I have nothing to hide nor revere

My walls are down, I'm no longer alone
My thoughts, my heart, I can now atone
Letting someone in is a personal choice
One that requires courage and trust

This is personal, a journey made with care
For it's only when I'm vulnerable, I can truly
share.

Metal Heart

Once upon a time, there was a young girl who
had a metal heart.
It was not made of flesh and blood, but of iron
and steel.
She was resilient and strong, but deep down she
was fragile and scared.

She had heard the stories of love, and of the
tenderness of a beating heart,
But her metal heart was cold and unyielding, and
she was weary of the world.

People would try to reach out to her, but she kept
her true self hidden away,
For the fear of being hurt or betrayed was
always there.

But one day, something changed within her.
She realized that her metal heart could be a
source of strength,
And she decided to open herself up to the world.

She embraced the love that she was given,
And her metal heart began to beat with the
rhythm of life.

She found joy in the simple moments,
And her metal heart grew warmer and stronger.

The world around her seemed brighter,
And her metal heart was no longer a barrier,
But a source of strength and courage.

The young girl learned to trust again,
And her metal heart became a symbol of her
resilience.

Though it may have been made of iron and steel,
Her metal heart was full of love and hope.
This is her story to tell.

Ink Stained Confessions

My ink-stained confessions, written in haste,
Letting out the words that I cannot face.
Amidst the fear and trembling, I set it all free,
A newfound courage I can finally see.

I'm writing of my thoughts, the joys and the
pain,
The secrets I've kept, that I loathe to explain.
My words come out so quickly, I'm barely
aware,
As I relive the moments that I'd rather not share.

My ink-stained confessions, the words that I
write,
It is a mixture of sorrow and joy that I fight.
The things I regret and the moments so sweet,
All laid out on paper I can't help but repeat.

My ink-stained confessions, a story of me,
The things that I've done that I wish I could flee.
The truth of my life, the things I have said,
I'm writing it all down, my ink-stained
confessions instead.

My ink-stained confessions, the pages I've
penned,
Are a reflection of the person I am in the end.
The joy and the sadness, the love and the fear,
All these things I must confront as I write about
here.

My ink-stained confessions, the truths of my
heart,
Are the stories I tell when I'm far apart.
Though I'm scared of the future, I must write
what I see,
For that is the only way I can set myself free.

Self Pity

In the depths of self-pity, a soul resides,
A heart burdened by dreams it cannot confide,
A yearning for greatness, yet tangled in doubt,
A prisoner within, unable to break out.
Oh, the knowledge of potential, so grand,
A fire within, waiting to be fanned,
But fear holds its grip, like chains around the
soul,
Leaving dreams untapped, unfulfilled, and
untold.
The world around, a flurry of motion and drive,
Each person striving, their purpose alive,
Yet here I stand, lost in the shadows of doubt,
Crying and whining, consumed by self-pity's
bout.
I know deep inside, there's a spark to ignite,
A greatness within, waiting to take flight,
But the path seems unclear, a maze of confusion,
Leaving me stagnant, trapped in this illusion.
Oh, how I despise this self-pity's embrace,
The tears and the whining, the feeling of
disgrace,
For I long to break free, to rise above the strife,
To embrace my potential and transform my life.
But the fear, it lingers, like a cloud in the sky,

Casting shadows of doubt, as the days pass me
by,
I question my worth, my purpose, my place,
Lost in the labyrinth of life's daunting race.
Yet deep down, I know, there's a warrior within,
A spirit resilient, waiting to begin,
To conquer the doubts, to silence the cries,
To soar beyond self-pity and touch the skies.
So, I wipe away the tears, and I stand up tall,
I refuse to be captive to self-pity's call,
For greatness awaits, and it's time to embrace,
The journey ahead, with courage and grace.
No longer will I wallow, in this pit of despair,
I'll rise from the ashes, with dreams to repair,
With each step forward, I'll find my own way,
No longer held prisoner to self-pity's sway.
For I am not defined by the doubts in my mind,
But by the strength and resilience I'll come to
find,
I'll embrace the unknown, with a spirit renewed,
And uncover the greatness that I always knew.
So, let the tears cease, and the whining subside,
As I embark on this journey, with purpose as my
guide,
No longer trapped in self-pity's embrace,
I'll break free, and let my greatness find its
place.

My skin

I look in the mirror, deep in my soul,
I see my black skin and it takes its toll.
Why is my skin judged so harshly and cruelly?
My pigment decides who I am in other's views.

It's not the clothes I wear or the way I speak,
It's my dark skin that decides my fate so bleak.
I look to the sky and ask why?
My black skin decides my worth and makes
others pass by.

My skin is beautiful and strong,
It's not a sign of weakness, it's a song.
My skin is my pride, I won't be denied,
My black skin is my identity and I will abide.

Caged Heart

A caged heart resides,
Where emotions are locked, where pain
coincides.
For I cannot bear the weight of their might,
So I lock them away, hidden from sight.

Oh, this heart of mine, once wild and free,
Now trapped in a cage, yearning to flee.
Its beats, like a bird, flutter and strain,
But I keep them contained, for I cannot sustain.

The bars that surround it, unyielding and cold,
A fortress of steel, a story untold.
Each emotion, a prisoner, longing for release,
But I fear their power, their relentless increase.

For if I were to let them roam free,
What chaos and turmoil would they decree?
So I keep them locked tight,
within my core,
And pretend that I'm fine, that I want nothing
more.

But deep down inside, in the crevices of my
being,

I know that this cage is not meant for fleeing.
It is a choice that I make, to keep going on,
To press forward, no matter how long.

For life is a journey, a path to be tread,
And though my heart's caged, I won't be misled.
I'll keep pushing forward, with a smile on my
face,
Hoping that someday, my emotions will find
grace.

In the face of adversity, I'll stand tall and strong,
Knowing that I am where I belong.
And maybe, just maybe, one day I'll find,
A key to unlock this heart of mine.

But until then, I'll keep it contained,
A caged heart, hidden and restrained.
For I am a warrior, unyielding and brave,
I'll keep pressing forward, emotions be saved.

What is Love?

What is this thing that people speak of?
A word so often used, yet never truly seen

Is love a feeling, a thought, an emotion?
A state of being, a state of heart, a notion?

For a young woman in her twenties never having
experienced it
Love can seem like an enigma, shrouded in
mystery and wit

Is love a feeling of butterflies in your stomach?
A warmth that radiates from within and never
succumbs?

Is love a thought, a hope, and a dream?
A longing for something that can't be seen?

Is love a state of being, a state of heart?
A state of mind that never seems to part?

Is love a notion, a concept, a thing?
A thing that can bring joy and yet, pain?

And so, here I stand, a young woman in her
twenties never having experienced it
I find myself asking, what is this thing called
love?

Tangles Thoughts

The memories of my past, they keep me bound
My mind is in a tangled web, no way to be
found
I try to piece together my thoughts, but they only
lead me astray
My heart is filled with fear, in the night I cannot
stay

My dreams become reality, and I am filled with
dread
For I am trapped in this web, and I cannot
escape instead
The more I try to free myself, the tighter the
knots become
My tangled thoughts are my prison, will I ever
be done?

I try to focus on the future, and on my newfound
strength
But the past keeps on creeping in, and I'm filled
with sadness and regret
My thoughts are a jumble, and I cannot seem to
find the way
To untangle my mind, and to free myself today

The more I work to unravel my tangled thoughts
The more I realize I must take the time and
pause
For I must look within myself and find the
courage to fight
To free my tangled thoughts, and be free in the
night.

Fragments of Silence

The world is a cacophony of sound,
A never-ending chorus of chaos that surrounds.
But amidst the chaos, I find solace in the silence,
A serene stillness that I embrace without
violence.

I find it in the morning dew,
It's a gentle whisper that soothes me anew.
In the night sky, stars sparkle and shine,
Their beauty so captivating, a sublime divine.

The wind blows through the trees,
A rustling sound that brings me ease.
The waves crash against the shore,
A ceaseless rhythm that I adore.

The chirping of birds in the early morn,
A symphony of love that I adorn.
The buzzing of bees in the lush green meadows,
A reminder of nature's beauty that never fades.

Even in the midst of the hustle and bustle,
The silence never ceases to exist as a subtle.
It's a reminder of the beauty of life,
A reminder to enjoy the moments of peace and
strife.

So, when the world is too loud and
overwhelming,
I close my eyes and let the silence be my
calming.
Fragments of silence, a beauty that can always
be found,
A reminder of life's peace that still abounds.

Slow Growth

She watches the world grow,
Stands still, alone in the snow.
She sees the stars above,
But her dreams still fail to move.

The people around her move ahead,
Their dreams soaring, she's filled with dread.
The future so far away,
The present is so gray.

The path ahead winding,
Her steps are so slow, binding.
She looks to the sky,
And her dreams begin to die.

But then a flicker of hope,
Her dreams begin to cope.
She takes her first step,
Her journey she sets.

She takes her time,
Grows in her own rhyme.
She watches the world and still stands tall,
Her dreams will bloom in the spring, after all.

Fairytale

The world tells me to keep my feet on the
ground,
To stop dreaming of a happy-ever-after,
But I can't help but to want a crown,
On a throne of joy, I'll laugh ever after.

The world tells me to set realistic goals,
To stop dreaming of a prince in shining armor,
But I can't help but feel that in my soul,
A fairytale is what I'll be living for.

The world tells me to live in the present,
To stop dreaming of a happily ever after,
But I can't help but feel content,
When I'm dreaming of perfect laughter.

The world tells me to face reality,
To stop dreaming of a fairy tale ending,
That's just a storybook ending
But I can't help but feel glee,
When I'm dreaming of life never-ending.

Social media

She scrolls, her eyes heavy,
As stories from her peers flash by.
Why can't she live that life, she wonders,
Her heart is full of envy and sighs.

Questions for God fill her head,
Though He reassures her instead.
"My plans for you are far greater,
Then what you can see on your screen."

The young woman takes a deep breath,
And closes her eyes in relief.
She can trust that God has her back,
Even if she can't see it yet.
A young adult woman, browsing the screen
Thoughts of envy, a life so serene
Why can't I have it, I often question God
But he whispers "Trust me, that life's a facade."

The lives of others, with wealth and fame
Their stories captivate, I'm stuck in a daze
Dreaming of a life, that I cannot obtain
But I'm reminded I have a different plan

God reassures me, His will will be done
My life will be special, just like the sun
I won't know it all, but I will be strong
A life of purpose, that can't be wrong.

Normal

What is normal? Is it what society says?
Is it what we as individuals feel?
Or is it what God has personally revealed?
We may not like the outcome, that much is real
But what is truly normal? That's the big deal

It's hard to define what is normal in this world
We're all so different and our stories are untold
But when we come together, it's a story to
behold
A story of unity, of beauty to be bold
That's when we know what is truly normal

Normal is not a rule or a law to abide by
It's a feeling and idea that we keep close by
When we can be free and be who we truly are
That's when we know what is truly normal by
far.

Fake

I have to fake how I feel,
To make someone else feel real,
Though I'm tired and weary,
I have to act like I should.

My true feelings I must not show,
For it will make them feel low,
The reality of themselves they must face,
And I must put on a smile in their place.

I must fake how I feel,
Even when I'm not doing well,
For if I show the truth of my heart,
It will tear them apart.

It's not easy to pretend,
To be something I'm not in the end,
But if it helps them to feel better,
Then I can pretend,
Until they can face reality again.

Motion's

Some days are a blessing, a joyous surprise
We bask in the beauty of life in the skies
Other days are a burden, a weight on our backs
We drag through the day, counting down the
minutes,
the hours, the days till we relax.

Average days come and go, without much ado
We just try to get through, with a bit of a clue
Boring days stretch on, with nothing to do
We wander the streets, searching for something
new.

We ponder the thought of life, of all its strange
twists
the best and the worst, the good and the bad,
all the highs and the lows, that we can't resist
No matter the turn of the tide, we must carry on
For life is a journey, that's never quite done.

Out of focus

My eyes have grown weary and heavy,
The world around me is a blur.
My vision is out of focus,
I'm in a fog, unsure.

My thoughts are muddled and hazy,
My emotions are so hard to bear.
My mind is out of focus,
Stuck in a state of despair.

The days blend together in confusion,
My future remains unclear.
My life is out of focus,
My worries I cannot hear.

But I know in time I will find clarity,
My vision will be restored.
My world will come into focus,
My strength will be restored.

Thoughts

Thoughts come and go like the wind
Drifting through my mind again
Sometimes I can barely contain
The myriad of thoughts I gain

Thoughts of laughter and joy
Thoughts of sadness and sorrow
Sometimes they come with no warning
Leaving me in a state of limbo

Thoughts of the future and the past
Thoughts of love that will last
Sometimes they come with a crash
Leaving me in an emotional mash

Thoughts of hope and of doubt
Thoughts of courage and fear
Sometimes they come with a boom
Leaving me lost in a fog so dense

Thoughts that come and go like the wind
Drifting through my mind again
But I know I can contain
The myriad of thoughts I gain

Not true

In a world of fantasy, I'm so grand
My life is filled with richness and glam
My house is made of gold and my car is a
gleaming Lamborghini
Money and fame are my only companions, never
a lonely night

In this world of make-believe, I'm so bold
My words are feared by all I behold
My wisdom is unrivaled, my power
unchallenged
My opinions are revered and my decisions never
questioned

In this alternate reality, I'm so wise
My knowledge is vast and ever-growing, no one
can surmise
My intelligence is limitless, my wit is so sharp
My ideas are revolutionary, my vision, a work of
art

In this land of fiction, I'm so majestic
My presence is felt by all, no one can be
sarcastic

My beauty is unparalleled, my charisma never
failing
My aura is a force of nature, its power never
waning

In this paradise of lies, I'm so perfect
No one can compare, no one can reject
My dreams come true, my heart never aching
In this place of make-believe, my life is truly
breathtaking.

Freedom

A person of wealth, with masked freedom
Living in a city, a prison unseen
The illusion of choice, the delusion of free
A life of privilege, a silent scream

A heart full of ache, a mind full of fear
A spirit that's broken, a soul that's so clear
The power of money, the chains of the elite
A life of pretending, a life incomplete

A society caged, a people oppressed
A world of suffering, a people distressed
Though freedom of thought, a right that's denied
A future of hope, a right that's denied

The power of money, the chains of the elite
A life of pretending, a life incomplete
Though freedom of thought, a right that's denied
A future of hope, the freedom we seek.

"Tears on a Windowsill"

A quiver on the lip of dawn, a chill upon the
glass,
Where misty sorrow clings to light, as shadowed
moments pass.
The windowsill, a barren perch for droplets of
despair,
A silent witness to loss, an echo of the prayer.

Tears fall like autumn's aching leaves upon the
stoic wood,
Each one a story of a dream that's gone where no
dream should.
They speak in hushed and saline tones of love
that's slipped away,
Of whispered nights and clasped hands now lost
in yesterday.

A child's laughter, once a stream, now but a
fading trace,
A mother's touch, a father's strength, vanished
without grace.
Here sits the mourner, gazing through the pane's
reflective eye,
A soul adrift in memories that never say
goodbye.

The world outside moves on and on, beneath the sky's grand sweep,
Unaware of the silent play, the eyes that cannot weep.
Yet in each tear that finds its rest on weathered, wooden sill,
Lies the heartache of a thousand woes that time can never still.

A portrait of the ones we've loved, a canvas wet with pain,
Each droplet holds a piece of us, a love we can't regain.
The tears they gather, merging in an endless, briny sea,
A flood of what has been before, and what can never be.

But look! A break within the clouds, a ray of hope's soft light,
Illuminating tear-streaked grief with warmth of morning bright.
What tales will these tears tell when kissed by sun's warm thrill?
Will they evaporate to sky or linger, chilly still?

The weeper by the window knows not what the morrow holds,

If tears will dry upon the sill or if the heart
enfolds.
A story's end, unwritten still, in salty trails we
find,
For tears on a windowsill leave deepest truths
behind.

Head in the Clouds

My head's in the clouds, as I gaze up above
Away from reality, in a world of love
Where birds soar and the sun shines bright
It's an escape from the stress of life

I take pictures of the sky, of beauty untold
The blue and the white, the shape of a crescent
moon's hold
The clouds forming patterns, like a masterpiece
of art
A reminder of the beauty, within our hearts

Away from the hustle and bustle of life
The worries and the strife
As I look up above, I'm filled with peace
As I take in the beauty, of the sky so deep

It's a chance to reset, and to reflect
On the beauty of life, and the things I neglect
To pause and appreciate, all the moments in time
To look up in the sky, and leave all my worries
behind.

The Weight of Worry

The quiet of the dawn, before the world awakes,
I count the costs of dreams, the risk each new
day takes.
A tapestry of thoughts, in tangled threads of
care,
Weighs upon my waking hours, a garment heavy
to bear.

The mortgage of the mind, with interest rates of
stress,
Compounded by the minute, a numerical caress.
Each bill, each chore, each deadline, like a stone
upon my chest,
In the ledger of my life, where worry comes to
nest.

Yet in this burdened breathing, a hopeful heart
resides,
For in the weight of worry, a resilient spirit
hides.
And though the load may not lighten, my back
grows strong and sure,
Carrying the common currency of thoughts both
rich and pure.

Reflections in the Stillness

In the stillness of the night, the world holds its breath,
A canvas blank and waiting, for the artist known as Death.
But in this quiet contemplation, where shadows softly play,
Life's brush strokes touch the canvas, in the gallery of the everyday.

A reflection of the moments, that dance like candlelight,
The laughter and the sorrow, the peace and then the fight.
A mindful observation, of the transient and the true,
A painting ever-changing, with every hue and view.

In the gallery of the everyday, where thoughts like patrons roam,
We find the art of living, in the museum we call home.
Contemplating quietly, the beauty that life bestows,
In the stillness of the night, where thoughtfulness quietly grows.

The Echoes of Loss

A silent scream in a crowded room, where no
one turns to see,
The echo of a heartbreak, that whispers,
"Remember me."
A chair that sits unoccupied, a voice that's heard
no more,
A shadow cast upon the floor, where light once
danced before.

The echoes of the laughter, the remnants of the
past,
Haunt the halls of memory, in a play that's ever
cast.
A longing for the touch, the warmth of a hand
now cold,
The story of a loss, in whispered thoughts retold.

Yet in these quiet echoes, where sorrow softly
weaves,
A tapestry of love remains, in the heart that
grieves.
For though the chair is empty, and the voice has
ceased to be,
The echoes of a life well-lived, are etched in
memory.

The Dance of Joy

The leap of a child, in the sun's warm embrace,
There's a rhythm of joy, a life-affirming grace.
A giggle on the wind, a skip without a care,
An open-armed surrender to the music in the air.

The simple things, a petal's blush, the sky's
expansive blue,
A dance of joy, a heart that sings, a world that
feels anew.
In every cherished moment, where happiness
resides,
Is the dance of life's sweet pleasure, where true
contentment hides.

So let us twirl with abandon, beneath the sun's
bright rays,
And let our laughter mingle, as we embrace the
day.
For in the dance of joy, no thought can take its
toll,
And happiness becomes the partner of the soul.

A Wisp of Doubt

The chamber of conviction, firm and stout,
Creeps silently a slender wisp of doubt.
A subtle thread, unseen in minds devout,
Weaving through belief, it takes its route.

It dances on the edges of the sure,
A spectral whisper, questioning and pure.
It tugs at certainties that once were pure,
And murmurs softly, "Are you truly sure?"

It's not a storm that rages, roars, and shouts,
But a silent mist that never fully flouts.
A ghostly hand that hesitates, then pouts,
It leaves the heart with questions and with
"doubts."

This wisp, this shade, this specter of the mind,
A sliver of the might of humankind,
To question what we've known, to seek and find,
A force that proves our thoughts are not
confined.

It pulls at threads of what we've woven tight,
Asking if our tapestry is right.
It haunts the scholar's deep research at night,
And challenges the artist's keenest sight.

Yet in its presence, growth is often found,
For in the soil of doubt, new truths are crowned.
It is the space where our minds are unbound,
Where the seeds of enlightenment are sound.

So let it linger, this soft wisp of gray,
A sign that we are living, thinking clay.
A testament that we will find our way,
Through questioning, we'll greet the light of day.

Echo of the Broken

A chorus of the shattered, in the silence they
dwell.
The echo of the broken, a symphony of sighs,
Wings of fractured dreams,
under the moonlit skies.

Each crack tells a story, a history etched in pain,
woven with tears, in every fiber, a stain.
The echo of the broken, it hums a haunting tune,
A ballad of the lost ones, beneath the waning
moon.

They speak in tender fractures, of love that
slipped away,
Of promises like glass, shattered in the fray.
The echo of the broken, it dances on the breeze,
A lilting, mournful cadence, between the
rustling trees.

Hearts once brimming with hope, now but
empty shells,
Echoing with the memories of their forsaken
spells.
The echo of the broken, it resonates so deep,
In the quiet moments, where the lonely secrets
are kept.

Yet within this brokenness, a quiet strength is found,
In every piece that's fallen, there's a light that bounds.
The echo of the broken, a testament to survive,
To the enduring spirit, that keeps the hope alive.

For every echo fading into the vast, endless night,
Carries within its sorrow, a future burning bright.
The echo of the broken, not a signal of the end,
But a message of resilience, a broken heart's amend.

The Awareness of Being

Amidst the vast and endless expanse of all that
is,
There stirs a gentle knowing, a subtle state of
bliss.
The awareness of being, a quiet, profound
breath,
That rises and falls with life, and even with
death.

Not bound by the flesh, nor held by the mind's
eye,
It's the essence of existence, that never truly
dies.
The awareness of being, it whispers to the soul,
A reminder of connection, that we are part of the
whole.

In the dance of the cosmos, where stars are born
and fade,
Our consciousness endures, in the grand
masquerade.
The awareness of being, the observer within the
play,
Watching the scenes unfold, in a timeless ballet.

It's the space between thoughts, where silence speaks so loud,
A canvas of serenity, untouched by the crowd.
The awareness of being, a river running deep,
In its waters, the reflection of the secrets we keep.

It's the pause in the heartbeat, the gap between the breaths,
A doorway to eternity, beyond the realms of death.
The awareness of being, a flame that burns so clear,
Illuminating the darkness, making the unseen appear.

In the mirror of the moment, where past and future cease,
There lies the quiet power of an everlasting peace.
The awareness of being, a gentle, enduring call,
To awaken to the now, the most sacred gift of all.

The Shadow of Fear

In the quiet corners of the quivering heart,
Lurks the shadow of fear, a dark and sly art.
It creeps through the alleys of uncertain minds,
Feeding on doubts, on the scraps it finds.

A shroud over daylight, a thief in the night,
Turning dreams into mist, out of sight.
The shadow of fear, a silent oppressor,
It's cold grip on a constant, uninvited confessor.

It whispers of failure, of loss and of pain,
A looping refrain, an unwelcome chain.
The shadow of fear, it distorts and it lies,
Painting the world in a despairing disguise.

It breeds in the pause, in the "what if" and
"might,"
A specter that chokes the soul's innate light.
The shadow of fear, a barrier, a wall,
A force that can make even giants feel small.

But look! In the heart where the shadow resides,
Is a light that is waiting, it's time to preside.
For the shadow of fear is a shapeless thing,
With no more power than the courage we bring.

Face it, embrace it, and see it dissolve,
With each step of resolve, watch the shadow
absolve.
For fear is a shadow, and shadows retreat,
In the presence of light, their retreat is complete.

So let us step forward, out from the shade,
Into the brightness, where life is remade.
The shadow of fear, let it be known,
Can only exist where light hasn't shone.

The Unaware

The souls of the Unaware, a silent song.
They walk in the mist of the day's busy throng,
Unseeing the right, unhearing the wrong.

Oblivious to the colors of a sunset's blaze,
Unmoved by the night's starry gaze.
The beauty of life passes by, unseen,
Unfelt the verdant of the grass so green.

In the cacophony of life, they find their peace,
In the mundane and familiar, their leases.
The laughter of children, the song of the birds,
To the Unaware, are but distant, muffled words.

They tread through the seasons without a
change,
In a world unvaried, narrow, and strange.
The stories of people, the tales of the land,
Are like grains slipping through a loosely
clenched hand.

The Unaware, in their bubble, safe and sound,
Where the depth of existence is seldom found.
Life's sharp edges are dulled, its flavors mild,
Each day a repetition, tamed and wild.

Yet, in the heart of an Unaware might sleep,
A spark waiting to leap from the deep.
For within each soul lies a curious eye,
A yearning for truth that never truly dies.

One day the veil may lift, and the sight
Will break into darkness, bringing light.
And the Unaware will awaken, astir,
To the vibrant life they once were.

Till then they walk, in their gentle daze,
Through life's intricate, unnoticed maze.
Unknowing the treasures each moment bears,
The beauty and sorrow, the joy and the cares.

So whisper to the Unaware,
Life is a gift, rich and rare.
May the slumber break, the spirit revive,
To embrace the wonder of being alive.

How Could You

How could you, in the gathering dusk,
Thread silence through the eye of trust,
When all I held, not chained, but free,
Was belief in an unspoken 'we'?

How could you, with a turn of hand,
Unwrite the script, unmake the plan,
While I stood watching, seams undone,
A story ending before it begun.

How could you, with no debt to pay,
Wander so lightly, far away,
Leaving echoes in your silent wake,
A hollow full of give-and-take.

How could you, in the shared daylight,
Cast our common dreams to flight,
Not through malice, nor intent,
But in mere absence, your presence was spent.

How could you, without a bond to break,
Still stir the embers of an ache,
Not owed allegiance, nor a claim,
Yet in your leaving, whisper my name.

How could you, unknowing, cause such rift,
As if your leaving were a gift,
And I, recipient of the void,
Found in the lack, the unalloyed.

How could you, owe nothing, yet inspire,
In the quiet embers, a smoldering fire,
A sense of loss for that never held,
In the silent stories we never tell.

How could you, and yet why not,
Move as you do, a free thought,
While I stand rooted, feeling the bruise,
Of an expectation I never could use.

I Hope It Hurts

I hope it stings, I hope it burns,
The way you scattered my concerns,
A wish upon a vengeful star,
Yet knowing that's not who we are.

I hope you feel a twist, a pinch,
For every time you made me flinch,
A mirror to reflect the pain,
But then I sigh, for what's the gain?

I hope the echo of my cries
Finds shelter in your alibis,
And in that hollow, may you hear
The cost of every fallen tear.

But then the heart, it intervenes,
Too tender, too unbroken, it seems,
It whispers of a higher road,
Where burdens shared lighten the load.

I hope it hurts, just like I bled,
A karmic dance, a twisted thread,
Yet, in the same erratic breath,
I fear the weight of such a death.

For if your heart were truly marred,
By all the ways mine's been scarred,
Would I not carry double pain,
Once for mine, and yours again?

So I retract the vengeful seed,
And look to heal, to intercede,
For hearts that care too much, too deep,
Find no solace in another's weep.

I hope it hurts, the thought alone,
But not the bone-crushing ache I've known,
For empathy's unyielding clutch
Declares my soul can bear that much.

I hope you know, I hope you see,
The growth that comes from agony,
Yet I'll not wish the fire's heart,
Upon you, no, I'll stand apart.

I hope it hurts, a fleeting thought,
A battle with myself I've fought,
For in the end, what justice serves,
If in the hurting, love unnerves?

I Can't Make You Love Me

I whisper to the darkness, confessing my silent
dream.
Your laughter haunts my memory, your smile
lights my way,
Yet you walk a path unknowing, as I watch you
day by day.

I can't make you love me, though my heart beats
so loud,
In the silence of my longing, beneath this heavy
shroud.
You move with grace and beauty, a vision so
divine,
But your eyes don't see the love, that's buried
deep in mine.

I trace your shadow lightly, with fingers made of
air,
In a world where you don't notice, a love that's
always there.
Your voice is like a melody, that lingers in my
mind,
But I can't make you hear it, no matter how
much I try.

I can't make you love me, though every wish I
weave,
Is tangled in the hope that someday you might
see.
The way my heart is aching, the dreams that
softly call,
But you're a distant echo, beyond this fragile
wall.

I'll cherish every moment, that you unknowingly
give,
In the corners of my heart, where my secret love
will live.
For I can't make you love me, though the stars
may fall,
In this quiet, unrequited, I'll love you through it
all.

I Can Only Take So Much

Behind a smile, I hide the storm, a tempest in
my soul,
A mask of calm composure, to keep me in
control.
Yet deep within, the waves crash hard, emotions
fierce and wild,
A heart that's breaking silently, a spirit
unrevealed.

I can only take so much, before the dam will
break,
Before the tears I've buried, form an unforgiving
lake.
Each laugh, each grin, a bandage, over wounds
that never heal,
Concealing all the anguish that I can't afford to
feel.

Anger is my armor, a shield against the pain,
A fire that burns within me, in a cold, relentless
rain.
With every word unspoken, with every tear
unshed,
The fury grows inside me, a beast that must be
fed.

I can only take so much, before the cracks appear,
Before the rage I harbor, becomes too loud to hear.
Each outburst, each explosion, a cry for some relief,
From the torment of emotions, that offer no reprieve.

In the quiet of the night, when shadows drape the sky,
The smile fades, the anger cools, and I'm left asking why.
Why must I wear this armor, why must I hide my truth,
Why can't I show the world the hurt that lies aloof?

I can only take so much, before I lose the fight,
Before the darkness swallows, the remnants of my light.
So I ask for understanding, for patience, and for grace,
As I navigate this tempest, with a smile on my face.

You Can Only Do So Much

You can only do so much,
like a river carving through stone,
until the jagged edges wear you down,
and the current pulls you under.

To hold another's sorrow in your hands,
to cradle their broken pieces,
hoping your warmth will mend the cracks—
you forget your own hands bleed.

The heart is a vessel, not a well,
and though it overflows with love,
there are limits to its depths,
boundaries to its giving.

You can only do so much,
before your light begins to dim,
before your breath becomes a whisper,
lost in the echo of their need.

To be a pillar, steadfast and true,
is noble, but even pillars crumble,
under the weight of too many storms,
under the burden of carrying another's sky.

You must remember to breathe,
to find your own ground,
to let the sun kiss your face,
and the rain cleanses your soul.

For you can only do so much,
before the shadow's claim your light,
before the giving becomes a taking,
and you lose yourself in the void.

So, love with all your might,
but let the winds of self-care guide you,
for you can only do so much,
and that, dear heart, is enough.

You're Allowed

You're allowed.

To feel the storm rage within,
to let tears carve rivers down your cheeks,
to laugh until your sides ache,
or to sit in silence, heavy and still—
you're allowed.

To walk away from what no longer serves you,
from shadows that cling to your heels,
to step into the unknown, trembling but bold,
or to stay, rooted, finding peace in familiar
ground—
you're allowed.

To not show up when the world demands your
presence,
to retreat into the sanctuary of self,
to rest, to heal, to simply be,
or to rise, shining, to greet the day—
you're allowed.

To be a symphony of contradictions,
a mosaic of broken and whole,
to carry the weight of your past

and the light of your dreams—
you're allowed.

In this vast, chaotic dance of life,
with all its messy, beautiful steps,
remember, always:
you're allowed to be human.

I have to I have to sink to swim

I have to, I have to sink to swim,
Dive deep beneath the surface, dim,
Where shadows dance and echoes fade,
In the silent depths where fears are made.

I have to let the water close,
Around my lungs, let currents pose
Questions I've been scared to face,
In this underwater place.

I have to feel the pressure rise,
The crushing weight, the silent cries,
Of dreams abandoned, hopes submerged,
In the tide where past and future merge.

I have to, I have to lose my breath,
To find the life beyond the death,
Of who I was, to be reborn,
In the ocean's cold embrace, forlorn.

I have to let the darkness near,
To understand what I hold dear,
To fight the monsters in the deep,
That haunts my thoughts, disturb my sleep.

I have to, I have to trust the waves,
To carry me through hidden caves,
To guide me to the surface bright,
Where I can breathe, where there is light.

I have to, I have to sink to swim,
To transcend the fear, the doubt within,
To rise again, renewed, alive,
From the depths where I learned to survive.

When I Learned the Value of
the Word Love

It was in the quiet moments,
not in the grand declarations,
that I began to understand
the weight of a single word:
Love.

Once, I tossed it like confetti,
glittering and light,
believing the sparkle
was enough to sustain.

But then came the silence,
the spaces between heartbeats,
where echoes of careless whispers
left shadows on my soul.

I learned love is not a feather,
not something to be flung
into the wind without thought.
It is a stone,
solid, grounding,
meant to be held with intention.

In the eyes of a friend
who stayed through the storms,
in the touch of a hand
that wiped away tears,
I saw love's true form:
a quiet, steadfast presence.

I began to sift through my lexicon,
weeding out the frivolous,
the empty, the hollow,
until what remained
was pure, was real.

Now, I speak it with reverence,
a sacred incantation,
reserved for moments
that deserves its grace.

For love is not a word to be squandered,
but a promise, a vow,
a bridge between souls,
built with care, with trust,
with the deepest parts of our hearts.

And in that understanding,
I found a new language,
one that honors the essence
of what it means to truly feel,
to truly live.

When I learned the value
of the word love,
I discovered the power
of meaning, of truth,
of connection that binds us all.

And in that revelation,
I found myself,
whole, complete,
forever changed.

Experience Becomes a Memory

Dawn, where the sky blushes awake,
we sit, breathing in the birth of a new day.
The first light, a tender touch on our faces,
is already slipping into the vault of memory.

At a barbecue, the sizzle and laughter blend,
family stories twisting through the air like
smoke.
We are here, now, but already these moments
are etching themselves into the soft clay of our
minds.
Quiet in our rooms, the world outside a distant
hum,
thoughts cascade like silent waterfalls.
Every solitary heartbeat, every whispered
thought,
is a thread woven into what was.

On a vacation, toes buried in the sand,
the ocean's song, a gentle lullaby.
We capture it all, snapshots in our minds,
knowing these peaceful pauses will soon be past.

A birthday candle flickers, a wish is made,

surrounded by faces that form the constellation
of our lives.
Joy and love, fleeting yet profound,
crystallize into memories that shimmer in the
dark.

Experience becomes memory, a bittersweet
alchemy;
moments slip through our fingers like grains of
sand.
Some sting with the sharpness of loss,
Others warm us with the glow of nostalgia.

Each second, a fleeting gift, a brushstroke on the
canvas
of our existence. We gather them, cherish them,
knowing that in the end, all we truly possess
are the memories we've made, the echoes of our
lives.

In this grand mosaic of human experience,
every laugh, every tear, every breath
is a piece of the puzzle, a line in the story
of who we are, who we've been, and who we
will become.

Evil

When darkness creeps and evil stirs,
And hatred fills my heart like fur,
I know I must act in faith,
And forgive the one who caused me pain.

I must remember that I'm not God,
And that I'm just a human flawed,
It's not my job to judge or hate,
But to love and forgive, even if it's too late.

It's hard to love the one who hurt me,
But I must remember to be merciful and free,
To forgive them like the Lord God does,
And show them love that truly soothes.

Motions pt 2

Some days are a blessing, a joyous surprise
We bask in the beauty of life in the skies
Other days are a burden, a weight on our backs
We drag through the day, counting down the
minutes, the hours, the days till we relax

Average days come and go, without much ado
We just try to get through, with a bit of a clue
Boring days stretch on, with nothing to do
We wander the streets, searching for something
new

We ponder the thought of life, of all its strange
twists
The best and the worst, the good and the bad, all
the highs and the lows, that we can't resist
No matter the turn of the tide, we must carry on
For life is a journey, that's never quite done.

Reconsider

When the world seems too much to bear
When the woes of life are everywhere
Take some time and take a break
Reconsider what your life can make

When the clouds blanket the sky
And your thoughts are in a tie
Take a deep breath and stop to think
Reconsider what life can bring

When the days seem so long
And everything seems so wrong
Stop and take time to reflect
Reconsider what life can perfect

When the darkness covers the light
And your future is out of sight
Look within and take control
Reconsider what life can hold

Crumbling

The walls are crumbling,
The roof is caving in,
The windows shatter,
As the raging wind

The dust is settling,
As the memories fade,
The foundation quakes,
As the building starts to sway

The walls are crumbling,
The structure is weak,
The cracks keep growing,
As the future looks bleak

But even in ruins,
The spirit remains strong,
It will rise again,
When the new dawn comes along.

All over the place

A whirlwind of chaos, a mad race
Living life in a blur
A constant flurry, a whir

A hustle and bustle, a blur of sights
My mind is all over, a jumble of lights
A muddled mess of thoughts and ideas
A world of confusion, I'm living in fear

A million voices, all talking at once
My head is spinning, my heart's on the run
No rest in sight, no time to slow down
I'm running around, my feet on the ground

A scattered mess of ideas and dreams
No time to sit, no time to breathe
My days are a blur, my nights a haze
I'm all over the place, my life in a daze.

Growing Up

As a child, I was so small and meek,
Every day, I took a peek,
In the world around me,
Ready to explore and be free.

As I grew, I embraced the change,
And made life my own strange game,
Every moment was a surprise,
Every day I looked towards the skies.

As a teen, I was full of life,
Living for the moments of pure delight,
Taking every opportunity to learn,
And growing every day in turn.

As an adult, I am still growing,
More and more knowledge I am knowing,
Each day brings new adventures,
Never ceasing to amaze and wonder.

Fighting

We are always fighting
For our rights, for our voices, for our lives
Struggling for justice, for freedom, for respect
Fighting for the future, for the truth, for what's
right

We are always fighting
The hate, the darkness, the ignorance
The violence, the prejudice, the double standards
The oppression, the lies, the injustice

We are always fighting
The battles within, and the battles without
The battles that seem too hard to win
But never give up, never surrender, always
fighting

We are always fighting
For love, for peace, for our dignity
For acceptance, for understanding, for kindness
For a better world, a better life, a better future
Fighting for all that's good, for each other, for
always.

Late Nights

Lying in my bed, the clock strikes twelve
The only sound in the silent night
I drift away to a dreamland of my own
Where I can be lost in thought

I think of the moments that I have taken for granted
The conversations that I should have had
The memories that I should have made
But never had the chance

I think of the days that have passed by
The people I have met and the places I have gone
The things I have learned and the things I have done
But never felt fully present

I think of the things I should have said
The apologies I should have made
The truths I should have shared
But were too scared to say

And in the still of the night, I am overcome with
emotion
As I realize the precious time I have wasted
The moments I could have been living
But instead were spent ruminating

It's in these late nights I find understanding
That life is too short to keep dwelling on the past
And that the only way to move forward
Is to cherish the present and savor each moment
That I am blessed with and never take it for
granted.

Laughter

Laughter, oh laughter, so sweet and so bright
Your power more precious than any of life's
delight
Your beauty is unique, your sound like no other
A gift that is given, no need to bother

The intricacies of your smile, a mystery to
behold
It lifts the spirit and relieves the soul
It's the sign of pure joy, a moment of bliss
The power to heal, to comfort and to kiss

Your presence gives comfort and brings hope
anew
Easing worries, lifting clouds of blue
Your light so bright, your warmth so real
A smile that can turn a heart of steel

Your power so powerful, your effect so great
Your ability to lift, no one can debate
A smile so true, a laugh that's loud
All the pain, all the hurt, it can all be allowed

Laughter, oh laughter, so sweet and so bright
Your power is more precious than any of life's
delights.

Snow flowers

Flowers in snow, a sight to behold
A beauty so pure, a sight to told
The shimmering white, a cold winter night
The flowers in snow, a wondrous sight

Their petals so soft, they glow in the night
Covered in snow, a breathtaking sight
The falling snow, creating a blanket of white
The flowers in snow, an astonishing sight

A world of color, a world of delight
The flowers in snow, a magical sight
The dark night sky, the snowflakes in flight
The flowers in snow, a glorious sight

A winter's night, a sight so bright
The flowers in snow, a beautiful sight
A moment of peace, a moment of delight
The flowers in snow, a spectacular sight.

Cold

In the cold, the night is still
The stars twinkle above, so bright
A chill that creeps in from the hill
And the moon glows, a silvery light

The trees whisper secrets in the dark
The snowflakes fall, a gentle kiss
The wind howls, an eerie lark
Hiding beneath a blanket of bliss

The icy chill brings a shiver
As nature's beauty surrounds me
The snowflakes quiver and quaver
On this winter night, I can see

The frozen lake glistens in the night
As my heart warms with wonder
The stars twinkle with delight
In the cold, I find solace and slumber.

How the Sunrise Makes Me Feel

The sky begins to glow, a fiery orange hue
The clouds take on a shade of pinkish hue
The stars slowly vanish, in the morning dew
As I watch the sun slowly rise from view.

The colors of the sky, they take my breath away
The clouds cast a peacefulness, to start my day
The warmth of the sun, it fills my heart with glee
As I take in the beauty of the morning's scenery.

The sun brings a hope, that's hard to explain
A fresh start for a new day, without any strain
A chance to look ahead, and start anew
Watching the sunrise gives me a feeling of
renewal.

And as the sun rises higher in the sky
The beautiful colors begin to slowly die
But the feeling of joy and hope, it still remains
As I watch the sunrise, and feel its beauty and
grace.

Beautiful Mind

My mind is a garden, full of beauty and grace
Filled with ideas, wonders, and a wondrous
embrace
A place of creativity, a place of thought
Where I can explore and never be caught

My mind is my sanctuary, a place I can escape
Where I can express all that I create
A place of self-reflection, a place of peace
A place of understanding, and a place to find
release

My mind is my refuge, a safe place to be
Where no one can harm me, and I can be free
A place of solitude, where I can dream
A place of beauty, a place of serenity

My mind is a beautiful place, a place of love and
light
That can never be taken, and will always be
mine to keep in sight.

Flower

The beauty of a flower
Growing in an empty field
A reminder that even in the darkness
There is still hope

The love between two people
The bond that can never be broken
A reminder that in the chaos of the world
There is beauty in simplicity.

I love you

The sweetest thing I'll ever do
Is whisper softly, I love you
My heart so full and true
That I'm filled with joy when I say I love you

The warmest thing I'll ever feel
Is the love in my heart that's so real
It brings me peace and joy so pure
When I express my love to you, that's for sure

The bravest thing I'll ever do
Is to tell you my love is true
My heart so open, with no fear
When I say I love you, I know it's sincere

The most beautiful thing I'll ever see
Is the sparkle in your eyes when I say I love you
The way you smile and light up the room
Makes me so happy I said I love you.

Thank You

A hundred thank yous I must give
To the one who let me live
The book I wrote from within
A burden I wanted to shed

The honesty I wanted to share
This would not have been possible without you
there
To help me put my heart on the page
And tell stories through my rage

Your kindness and support I can never repay
But this book was a way to express what I could
not say
Your kindness I'll never forget
And for that I thank you with every breath

Thank you for the space and time
You made my dreams real, in just a rhyme
You gave me a book of my inner thoughts
And for that I thank you with all I've got.